Fold Yourself Calm

ORIGAMI

igloobooks

Published in 2016
by Igloo Books Ltd
Cottage Farm
Sywell
NN6 0BJ
www.igloobooks.com

Cover designed by Nicholas Gage
Interiors designed by Simon Parker
Edited by Natalie Baker

Cover images: © iStock

LEO002 0816
2 4 6 8 10 9 7 5 3 1
ISBN: 978-1-78670-206-7

Printed and manufactured in China

Contents

The Art of Origami

The History of Origami

Origami is the traditional Japanese art of paper folding, 'ori' meaning to fold and 'kami' meaning paper. Usually without any gluing or cutting, the paper is transformed by a series of folds into beautiful miniature sculptures: flowers, animals, birds, and festive decorations.

The art of origami was originally associated with Japanese religious ceremonies. Little origami sculptures would often be attached to gifts at weddings and other celebrations, just like a small decorative card might be today. Origami was then taken up as a creative hobby by the wealthy, who were able to afford the high cost of paper. As the price of paper dropped, origami became far more widespread and demonstrations of paper folding became a common form of entertainment in Japan, loved by adults and children alike.

The joyous, relaxing nature of origami means that the art is now a popular pastime not just in Japan, but throughout the world.

Learning the Art

Beautifully presented, this book gives you the opportunity to experience the exquisite art of origami yourself. Just a little practice at the basic folds and you'll soon progress to making your own amazing paper sculptures. Majestic tigers, glorious roses, flawless diamonds – there are over thirty models in all, each coming with clear step-by-step instructions. This book also provides the special squares of paper for all the models, each sheet appropriately patterned and colored. Everything is here for you to create your own stunning representations of the world's most beautiful animals, flowers, and treasures.

The Basics of Origami

Origami involves applying a series of folds to a square of paper to produce a miniature sculpture, which can be both incredibly intricate and lifelike. The instructions for each step in the modeling usually take the form of brief text with a special type of diagramming known as the Yoshizawa-Randlett system, devised by two origami enthusiasts. No glue is required and only very occasionally the use of scissors. It's all in the clever folding.

There are a variety of folds employed in origami: some very straightforward and some a little more complex.

The main types of fold are described and illustrated on the next few pages and it's a good idea to practice these on scrap squares of paper, before progressing to the specially colored and patterned squares that accompany this book.

The key to good origami is carefully aligned folds, with nice sharp creases. The less exact your folds, the more your model will stray from what you're hoping to create. Take care with your folds, give time to them, and your simple square of paper will start to magically transform into an amazing sculpture.

Folding instructions

The diagrams below show the various folds used for each model in the book. We've grouped them in the following categories: simple, more complex, and useful instructions.

 ## Mountain Fold (Simple)

Fold paper backwards, behind itself, to create a ridge-like crease.

 ## Valley Fold (Simple)

The most common type of fold. Fold paper forwards to create a valley-like crease.

 ## Point to Point (Simple)

Fold the paper so the two indicated points align.

 ## Fold and Unfold (Simple)

Fold, then unfold the paper to create a crease.

 ## Accordion Fold (Simple)

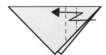

Fold the paper back on the 1st crease, then forward on the 2nd, to create a zigzag.

 ## Squash Fold (Complex)

Lift indicated crease and then squash down on top left corner to reshape that segment into a flattened diamond.

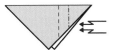

Inside Crimp Fold (Complex)

Fold the corner underneath at the 1st crease, then forwards at the 2nd, so it is hooded.

 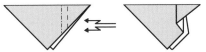

Outside Crimp Fold (Complex)

Fold the corner backwards at the 1st crease, then forwards at the 2nd, so it forms a hood.

Inside Reverse Fold (Complex)

Push top corner down so it protrudes from the inside of the crease.

Outside Reverse Fold (Complex)

Fold the top corner back on the crease so it is turned inside out and facing backwards.

Pull (Useful instructions)

Pull the corner of the paper in the direction indicated to remove the folds.

  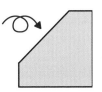

Turnover (Useful instructions)

Turn the paper around so you are now working on the back.

Repeat (Useful instructions)

Repeat an action. The number of lines on the arrow tells you how many times it is to be repeated.

 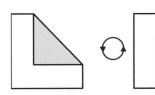

Rotate (Useful instructions)

Rotate the paper to match the diagram.

Let's get folding!

Practice pages

Start your origami practice with two relatively easy models. On the following pages we've provided all you need to make two beautiful animals – an Angel Fish and an Owl. The difficulty rating is shown top right and don't forget to refer back to the guide on pages 8–9 to refresh your memory on folding instructions. On page 17 there are some practice sheets to experiment with, so don't worry if you get it wrong the first time!

Paper patterns printed on both sides for all of the models start on page 112 and the correct paper for each origami model is identified top right.

Difficulty:

Angel Fish

1. Start with blank side of paper. Mountain fold along one dotted line, then the other. Now unfold and turn over.

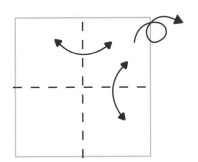

2. Mountain fold along each of diagonals, then unfold.

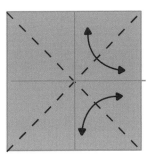

3. Push in on the left and right sides to form a triangle.

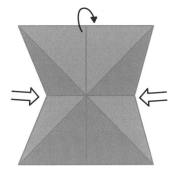

4. Valley fold right side of triangle along the dotted line.

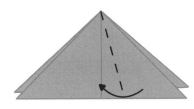

5. Valley fold left side of triangle against edge of right side.

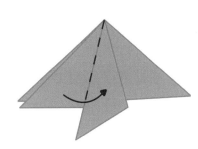

6. Turn over and you have a beautiful angel fish complete with a tail!

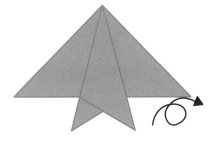

11

Difficulty:

Owl

1 Start with blank side of paper. Valley fold along dotted lines, then unfold.

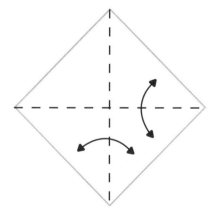

2 Valley fold top corner along the dotted line.

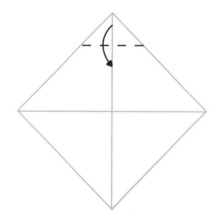

3 Valley fold bottom corner so that it just touches folded-down top corner.

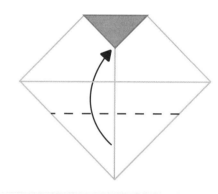

4 Valley fold left corner along the dotted line.

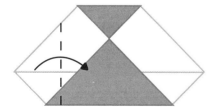

5 Valley fold right corner so it just touches fold in left corner.

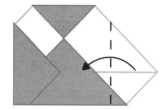

6 Valley fold along the dotted line to form beak. Draw on eyes!

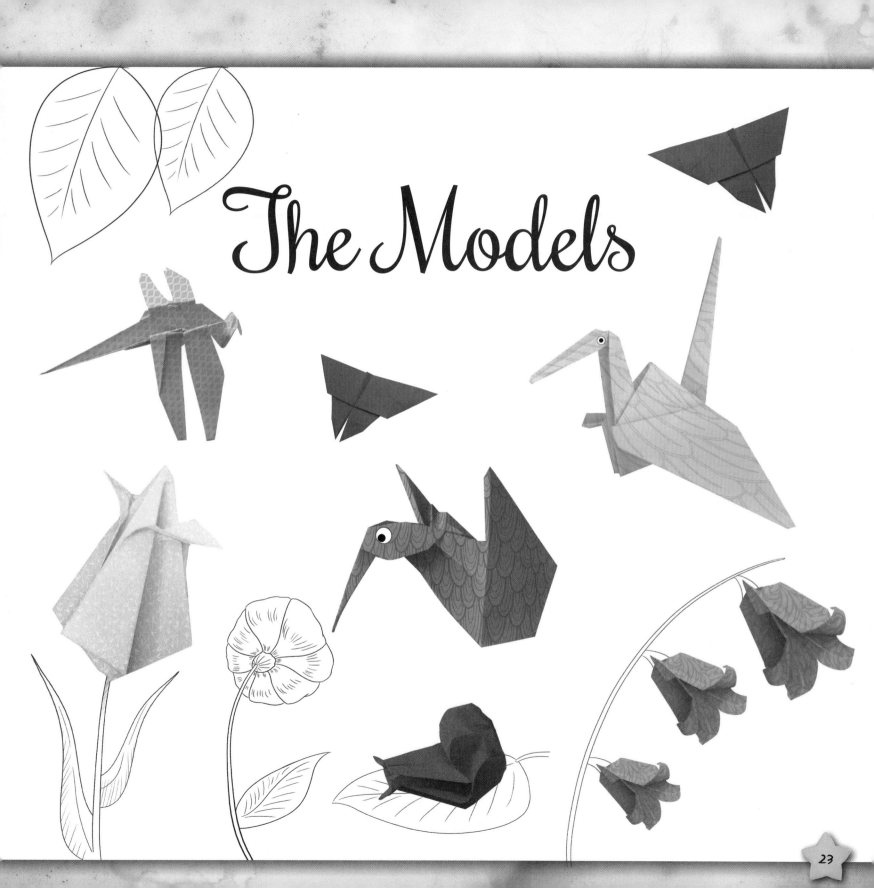

The Models

23

Buttonhole Flower

1 Start with lighter side of the paper. Fold and unfold along the dotted lines. Turn over.

2 Fold and unfold along the diagonal dotted lines.

3 Pull the top edge of the paper down while pushing the sides inwards.

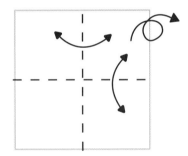

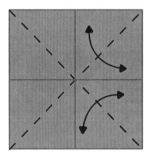

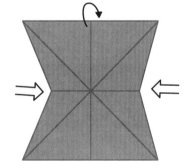

4 Fold the flaps from left to right creating a smaller triangle.

5 Fold back along the dotted lines.

6 Make sure that the point sits between the four triangles.

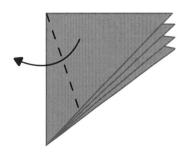

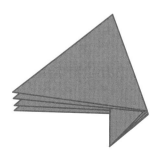

7   Hold the stem and rotate the model evenly spacing the triangles.

8   Open each triangle from the top to reveal the petals.

9   Shape the petals, by bending the tips backwards.

10

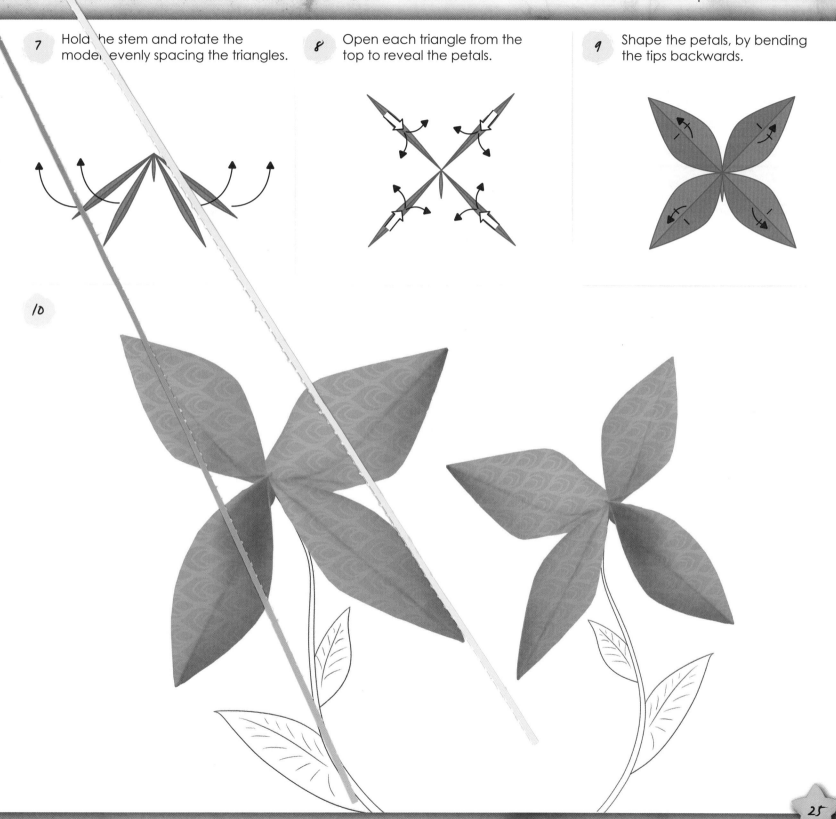

Difficulty:

Carnation

1. Start with lighter side of the paper. Fold and unfold along the dotted lines. Turn over.

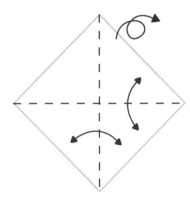

2. Fold and unfold along the dotted lines.

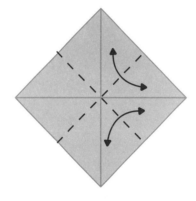

3. Push each corner inwards allowing the paper to fold into a diamond shape.

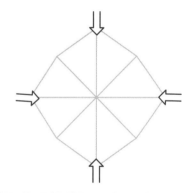

4. Fold the left flap to the center.

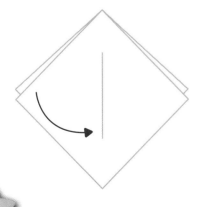

5. Pull apart the two layers of paper.

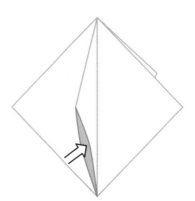

6. Flatten in the center.

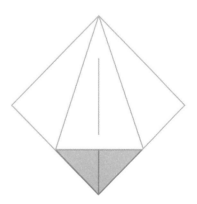

7 Repeat step 6, folding all remaining flaps to create a kite shape.

8 Fold all four pointed corners upwards along the dotted line.

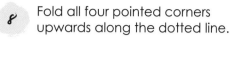

9 Arrange the paper so that there are four flaps on each side and fold backwards in half.

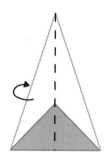

10 Push the triangle tip down, sitting between the eight flaps.

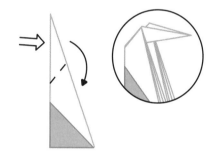

11 Disperse the paper flaps evenly to create the petals.

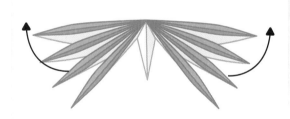

12 Pull apart the paper layers to shape the petals.

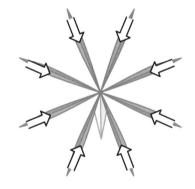

13

Difficulty:

Tulip

1 Fold the paper from corner to corner.

2 Fold in half again.

3 Unfold, then fold the square in half.

4 Open the square and fold along the dotted lines.

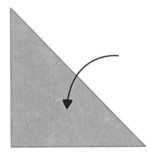

5 The origami model should look like this.

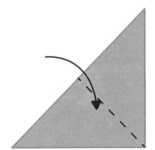

6 Fold the bottom corners of the top flap towards the top point.

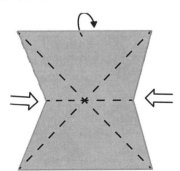

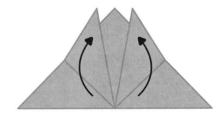

7   Turn over and repeat step 6.

8   Fold the top left flap inwards along the dotted line. Flip over and repeat on the other side.

9   Fold the corners into the middle crease.

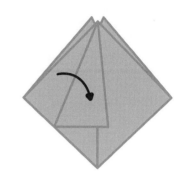

10   Repeat for all four corners.

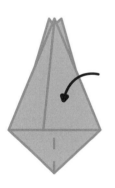

12

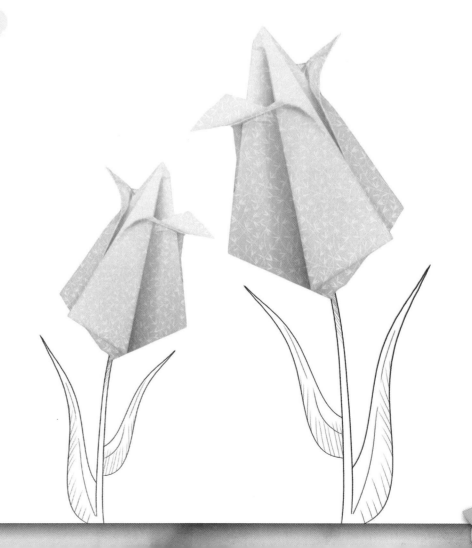

11   Gently pull the tips of each triangle out to create the petals.

Difficulty:

Rose

1. Start with darker side of the paper. Fold and unfold vertically along the center. Turn over.

2. Fold and unfold horizontally along the center.

3. Fold the four corners inwards along the dotted lines.

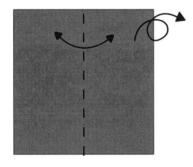

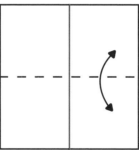

4. Repeat step 3.

5. Fold once more along the dotted lines.

6. Fold each corner backwards along the dotted lines.

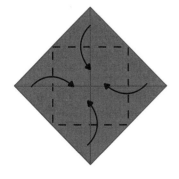

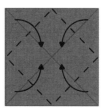

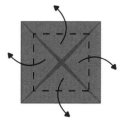

7 Repeat step 6.

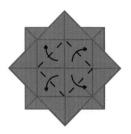

8 Repeat again.

9 Fold backwards along the dotted lines.

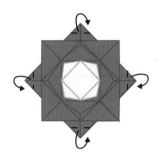

10

Difficulty:

Water Lily

1. Start with lighter side of the paper. Fold and unfold along the dotted lines. Turn over.

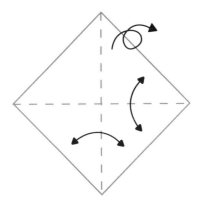

2. Fold inwards along the dotted lines.

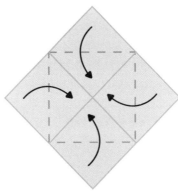

3. Repeat step 2, then flip over.

4. Fold inwards along the dotted lines.

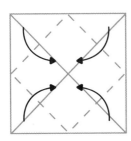

5. Your model should look like this.

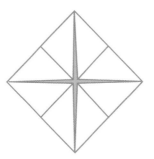

6. Unfold the top two flaps.

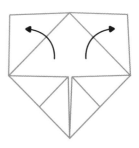

7 Swing the triangle flap forwards.

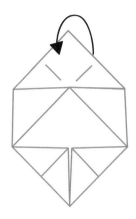

8 Push the two sides inwards allowing the triangle flap to fold forwards.

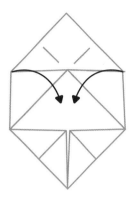

9 You have created the first petal.

10 Repeat steps 7–9 to form the remaining petals.

12

11 Pull the four hidden flaps forwards.

Bluebell

1 Fold and unfold along the dotted lines. Turn over.

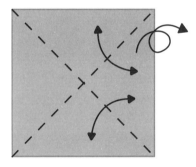

2 Fold and unfold along the dotted line.

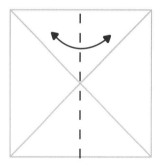

3 Fold downwards.

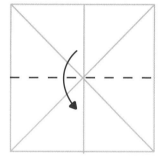

4 From the center line on the triangle, pull the top layer upwards.

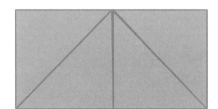

5 Push the bottom corners inwards, while lifting the center point.

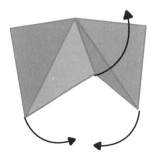

6 Allow the same folds to fall in place on the back.

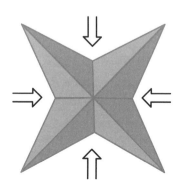

7 Flatten to create a diamond shape.

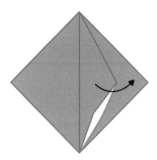

8 Fold the corners inwards along the dotted lines.

9 Unfold.

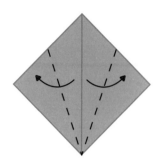

10 Pull open the top right flap.

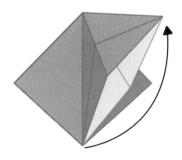

11 Push the paper inwards along the dotted lines.

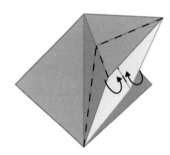

12 Flatten the fold.

13 Flip over.

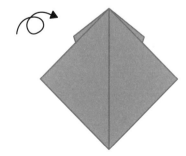

14 Fold the corners inwards along the dotted lines.

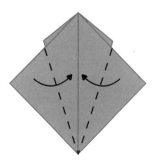

15 Unfold.

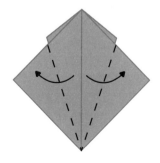

16 Pull open the top right flap.

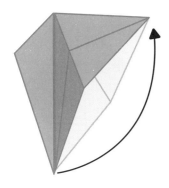

17 Push the paper inwards along the dotted lines.

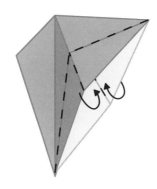

18 Flatten and repeat steps 14–17 on the remaining two sides to create a kite.

19 Fold inwards along the dotted lines.

20 Flip over.

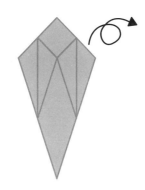

21 Repeat steps 20–21 for the remaining 3 sides.

22 Disperse flaps to create a 3D shape.

23 Pull apart to open.

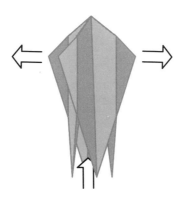

24 Rotate and shape flower.

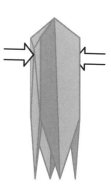

25 Pull the petals backwards.

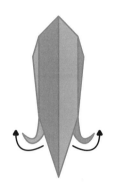

26 Rotate 90 degrees.

27 Shape remaining petals.

28

Difficulty:

Camellia

1 Start with lighter side of the paper. Fold and unfold along the dotted lines.

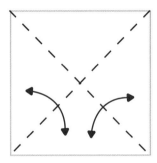

2 Fold and unfold in a diagonal line from the corner.

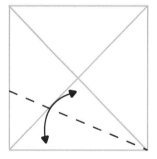

3 Fold again, along the dotted line.

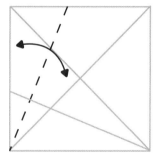

4 Repeat step 3.

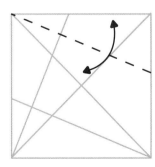

5 Fold and unfold the remaining corner along the dotted line.

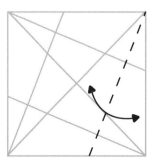

6 Fold along the dotted line.

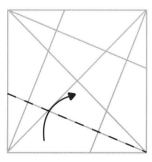

38

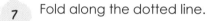

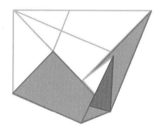

7 Fold along the dotted line.

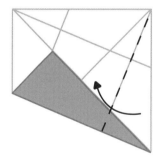

8 Fold the top layer of paper up along the dotted line.

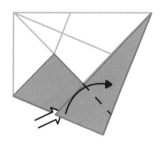

9 Flatten down.

10 Rotate and fold along the dotted line.

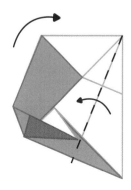

11 Fold along the dotted line (see step 9).

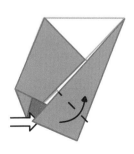

12 Rotate, then fold and unfold along the dotted line.

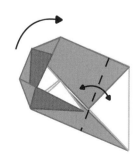

13 Lift the corner.

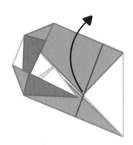

14 Flatten.

15 Fold the bottom right triangle inwards and flatten the top right corner.

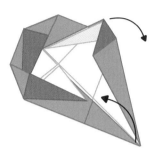

16 Fold along the dotted line and tuck underneath the top right corner.

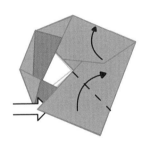

17 Your model should look like this.

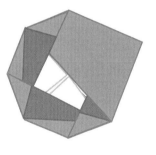

18 Flatten the model.

19 Rotate and fold upwards along the dotted line.

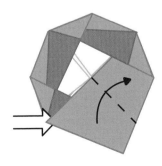

20 Tuck the exposed flap underneath the top right corner.

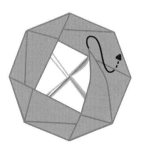

21 Fold back along the dotted lines.

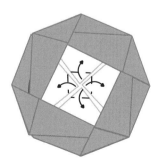

22

Difficulty:

Iris

1 Start with lighter side of the paper. Fold and unfold along the dotted lines. Turn over.

2 Fold and unfold along the dotted lines.

3 Push the top downwards allowing the sides to fold inwards.

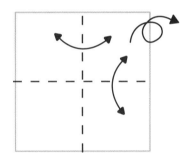

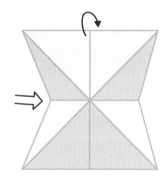

4 Flatten into a triangle.

5 Fold and unfold along the dotted line.

6 Open along the fold to create a pocket.

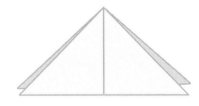

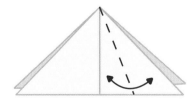

7 Flatten.

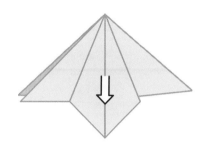

8 Repeat steps 5–7 so that the paper forms a kite shape.

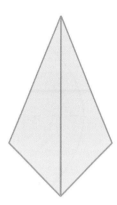

9 Fold along the dotted lines.

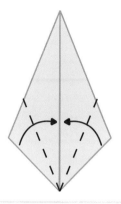

10 Open to create pockets, flatten and then fold back.

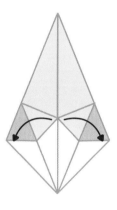

11 Fold in half and unfold.

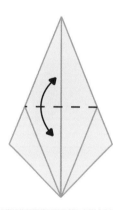

12 Lift the top layer of paper upwards.

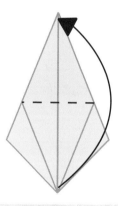

13 A pocket will form.

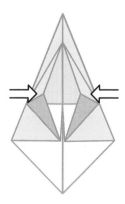

14 Flatten.

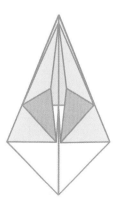

15 Your model will look like this.

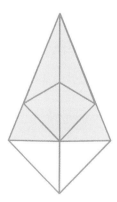

43

16 Pull the flap down.

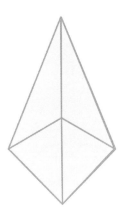

17 Fold along the dotted line.

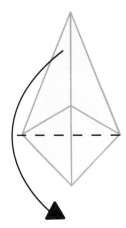

18 Rotate.

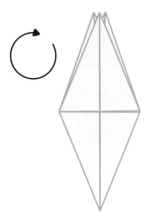

19 Fold along the dotted lines.

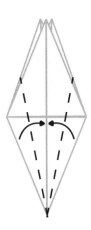

20 Rotate.

21 Fold all corners inwards.

22 Pull open the layers from the top point to reveal the leaves.

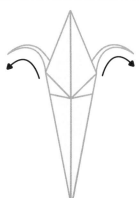

23 Rotate.

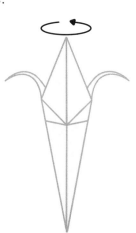

24 Shape the remaining petals.

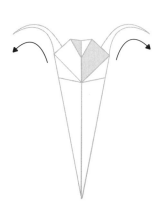

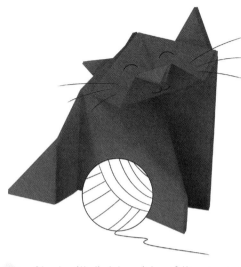

Cat

1   Start with lighter side of the paper. Fold and unfold along the dotted line.

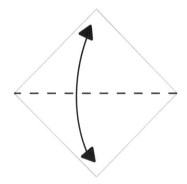

2   Then fold in half along the dotted line.

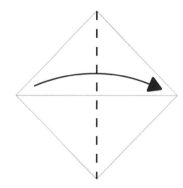

3   Fold top and bottom points inwards along the dotted lines.

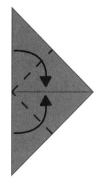

4   Fold in half.

5   Next, open the middle flap to form a pocket and allow the top flap to fold backwards. Flatten the fold.

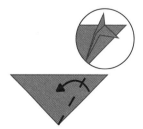

6   Rotate the model 45 degrees.

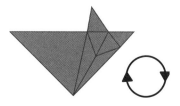

7 Fold the left tip inwards along dotted line to form the tail.

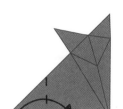

8 Fold the top left point behind itself and back along the dotted lines to create an ear.

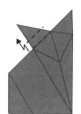

9 Repeat step 8 on the top right point.

10 Fold along the dotted line to create the face.

11 Fold along the dotted line to create the nose.

12

Difficulty:

Dog

1. Fold and unfold along the dotted lines.

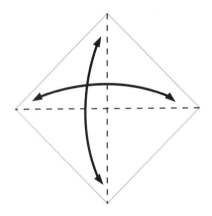

2. Fold along the dotted lines to make a square.

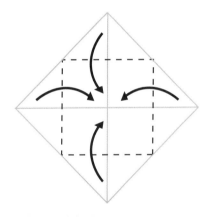

3. Open the left flap.

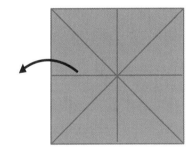

4. Fold the model in half along the dotted line.

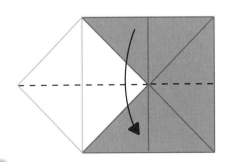

5. Fold along the dotted line so the flap swings forwards.

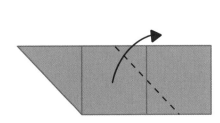

6. Open the flap to create a flap and flatten the fold.

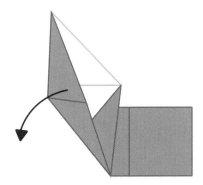

7   Fold along the dotted line.

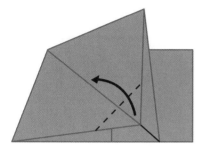

8   Fold along the dotted lines to create the ears.

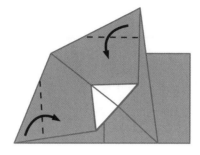

9   Fold along the dotted line to create the nose.

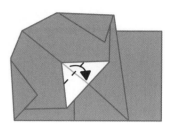

10   Fold the bottom right corners inwards to create a base.

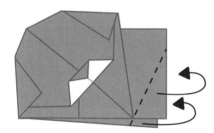

11   Rotate the model so it stands up.

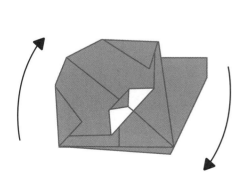

12

Mouse

1. Start with lighter side of the paper. Fold along the dotted lines.

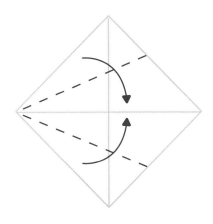

2. Fold and unfold along the dotted lines.

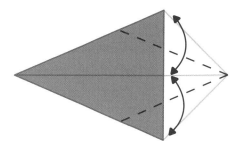

3. Push the straight edges forwards, allowing the paper to fold over the dotted lines.

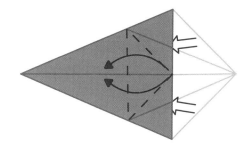

4. Fold backwards along the dotted lines.

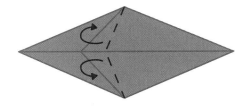

5. Fold the left corner of the kite shape backwards.

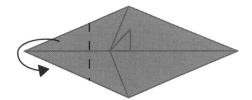

6. Fold backwards along the dotted line.

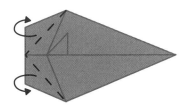

50

7 Fold backwards in half.

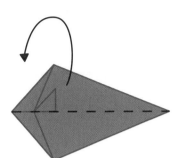

8 Fold downwards along the dotted line.

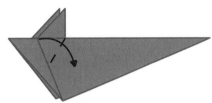

9 Pull open to create a pocket and flatten.

10 Turn the model over.

11 Repeat steps 8 and 9 on the other side.

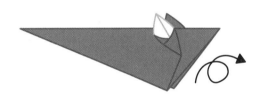

12 Push the corner down so that it slots inside the fold.

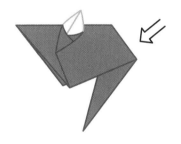

13 Fold the tip back again using the same technique.

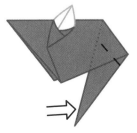

14

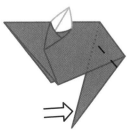

Bear

1 Start with lighter side of the paper. Fold and unfold along the dotted lines.

2 Fold inwards along the dotted lines.

3 Fold inwards along the dotted lines.

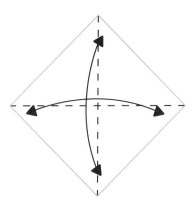

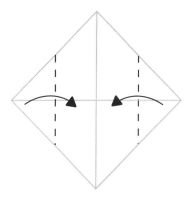

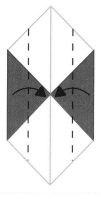

4 Unfold the paper.

5 Fold inwards along the dotted line.

6 Fold backwards along the dotted line. Repeat steps 6 and 7 on the other side.

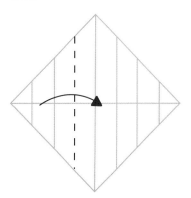

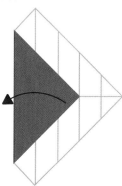

7   Fold the outer flaps up along the dotted lines.

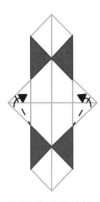

8   Pull the two bottom points outwards and fold the bottom flap along the dotted line. Flatten the fold.

9   Fold along the dotted line.

10   Fold along the dotted lines to create the arms.

11   Fold the top flap inwards along the dotted line.

12   Fold backwards along the dotted lines.

13   Make inside reverse folds on the top corners to make the ears.

14   Fold the model back a little to help it to stand.

15

Difficulty:

Elephant

1 Start with lighter side of the paper. Fold along dotted line, then unfold.

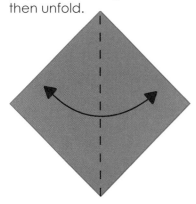

2 Fold each edge along dotted line.

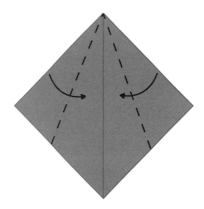

3 Turn over.

4 Fold top point down along dotted line so that it faces in the other direction.

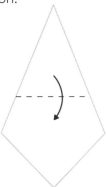

5 Fold along dotted line.

6 Turn over.

7 Fold the bottom point up along the dotted line.

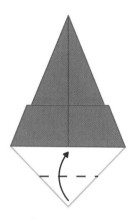

8 Fold in half.

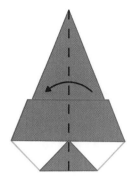

9 Fold down along the dotted line.

10 Fold up along line.

11 Push the corner down so that it slots inside the fold.

12 Fold the tip back again using the same technique.

13 Use the same technique on the tip to complete the trunk.

14 Rotate the model as shown, then cut along the dotted line to make the legs.

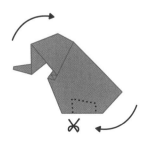

15

Difficulty:

Raccoon

1 Start with lighter side of the paper. Fold and unfold along the dotted lines.

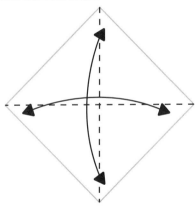

2 Fold inwards along the dotted lines.

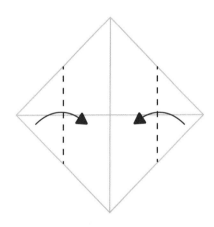

3 Fold inwards along the dotted lines.

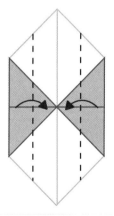

4 Unfold the paper.

5 Fold inwards along the dotted line.

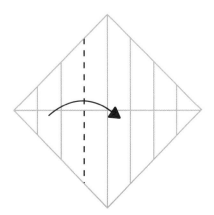

6 Fold backwards along the dotted line.

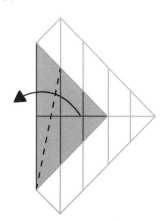

7 Repeat step 5.

8 Repeat step 6.

9 Fold inwards along the dotted line.

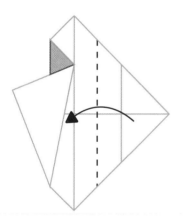

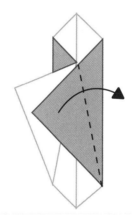

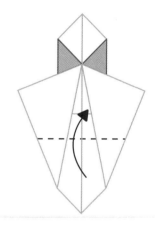

10 Fold down along the dotted line.

11 Fold inwards along the dotted line.

12 Repeat step 11.

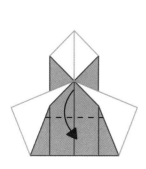

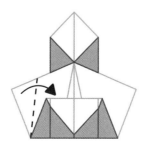

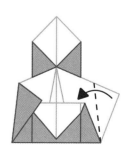

13 Fold and unfold along the dotted line.

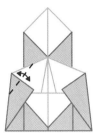

14 Repeat step 13.

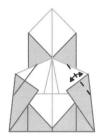

15 Pull flap outwards to create a pocket. Flatten the fold.

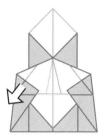

16 Repeat step 15.

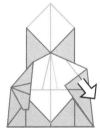

17 Fold the top flap down along the dotted line.

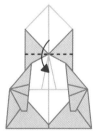

18 Make two inside reverse folds on the top corners to make ears.

19 Fold along the dotted line.

20 Fold along the dotted line to create a nose.

21 Fold backwards along the dotted lines.

22

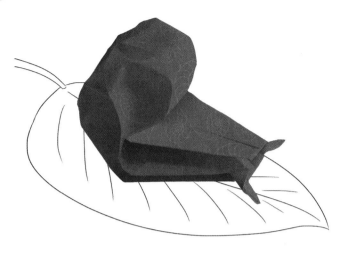

Difficulty:

Snail

1 Start with lighter side of the paper. Fold in half.

2 Fold in half again.

3 Lift the top triangle and open the pocket.

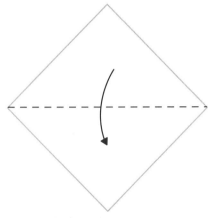

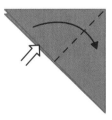

4 Flatten to create a square. Flip over.

5 Lift the triangle and repeat steps 3–4 to create a square.

6 Lift the top flap and open the pocket. Flatten the fold.

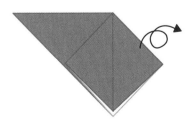

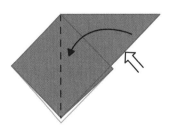

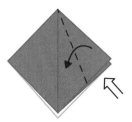

7 Repeat step 6 on the other three flaps.

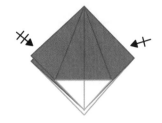

8 Rotate the model.

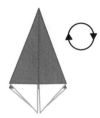

9 Fold the top flaps so the corners meet in the middle. Flip the model over and repeat on the other side.

10 Fold the middle flap over. Flip the model over.

11 Fold the middle flap over, then repeat step 9.

12 Fold the top flap over. Flip the model over.

13 Fold the top flap over.

14 Your model should look like this.

15 Gently pull out the middle tips a little.

16 Make a reverse fold on each tip.

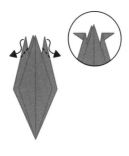

17 Fold the tip behind itself on the dotted line.

18 Pull the tips up to create antennae.

19 Fold the bottom tip over and tuck behind the antennae.

20 Fold model over at the dotted line.

21 Unfold the top flap so it stands upright.

22 The model should now look like this.

23 Pull out the inside pleats to bulge out the shell.

24 Pull out the outside pleats to finish bulging out the shell.

25

Difficulty: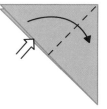

Frog

1 Start with lighter side of the paper. Fold in half along the dotted line.

2 Fold in half again.

3 Open pocket by folding the top triangle to the right.

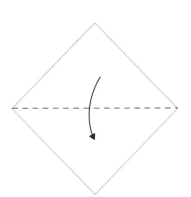

4 Flatten the fold. Flip over.

5 Repeat steps 3 and 4.

6 Lift the top flap and open the pocket. Flatten the fold.

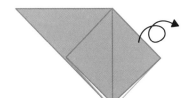

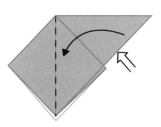

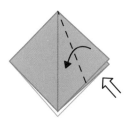

7 Fold pocket up along dotted line. Flatten the fold.

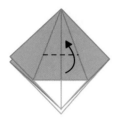

8 Flip over. Repeat steps 6 and 7.

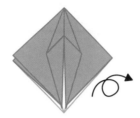

9 Fold flap behind in half. Flip over.

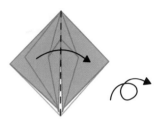

10 Fold flap behind in half and repeat steps 6, 7, and 8.

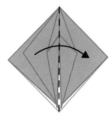

11 Fold along the dotted lines so the corners meet in the middle.

12 Fold in half upwards.

13 Fold along the dotted line.

14 Pull tip out gently.

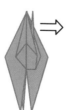

15 Open up the left flap by folding along the dotted line.

16 Repeat steps 11 to 14.

17 Flip over.

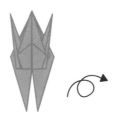

18 Fold along the dotted line.

19 Fold along the dotted lines so the corners meet in the middle.

20 Fold along the dotted line to make the back leg.

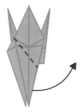

21 Fold the leg downwards along the dotted line.

22 Fold top flap over along the dotted line, and repeat steps 19 to 21 on the left leg.

23 Fold each tip behind itself to create hands and feet.

24 Fold top tip behind itself to create the face.

25

Difficulty:

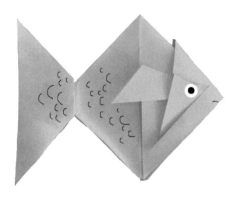

Tropical Fish

1 Start with lighter side of the paper. Fold in half.

2 Fold in half again.

3 Fold along the dotted line to form a diamond shape.

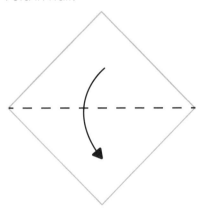

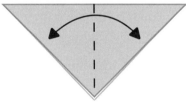

4 Fold the top layer of paper upwards along the dotted line.

5 Fold along the dotted lines.

6 Fold the bottom point upwards.

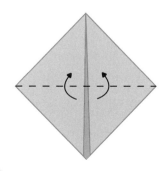

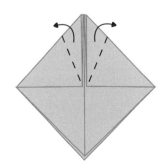

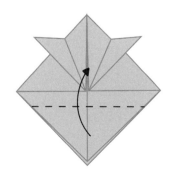

7 Fold upwards along the dotted line.

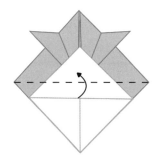

8 Cut along the dotted line with scissors.

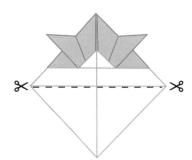

9 Now fold the lower half of the shape backwards.

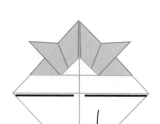

10 Push all three sides together.

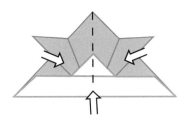

11 Rotate.

12 Pull the right side of the paper backwards from the center point, along the dotted lines.

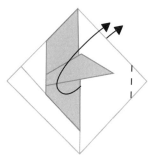

13

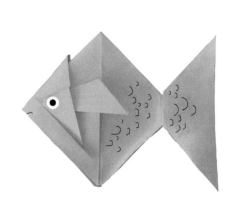
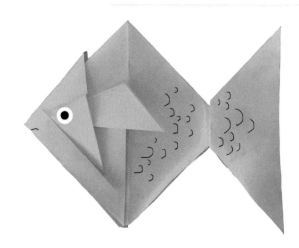

Sea Lion

1. Fold and unfold in half, then fold along the dotted lines to create a kite shape.

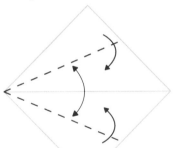

2. Fold along dotted lines so the top and bottom tips meet in the middle.

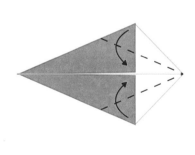

3. Your model should look like this.

4. Open up the top flap to create a pocket and flatten the fold. Repeat on the bottom.

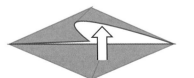

5. Fold the model in half behind itself.

6. Make an inside reverse fold along the dotted line.

7   Make an inside reverse fold along the dotted line.

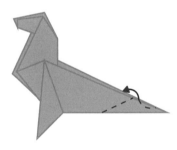

8   Fold the tip in on itself to make the face.

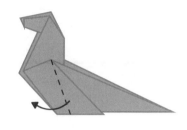

9   Fold the top flap along the dotted line to make the flipper. Repeat on the other side.

10   Make an inside reverse fold along the dotted line to create the tail.

11   Fold the flipper along the dotted line. Repeat on the other side.

12

Difficulty:

Crab

1 Start with lighter side of the paper. Fold in half.

2 Fold in half again.

3 Open the top left corner of the paper.

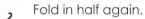

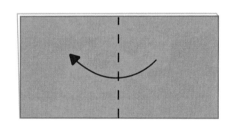

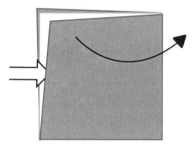

4 Pull to the right to create a pocket and flatten.

5 Flip over.

6 Repeat steps 3 and 4 on the right flap.

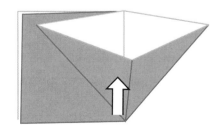

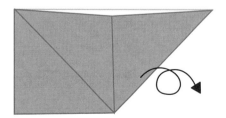

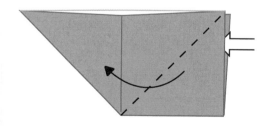

7 Fold the top layer behind itself along the dotted lines.

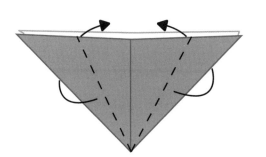

8 Flip over.

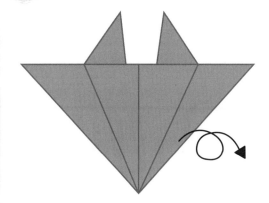

9 Fold along the dotted line.

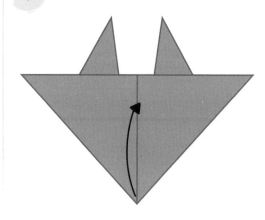

10 Fold inwards along the dotted lines to shape the claws.

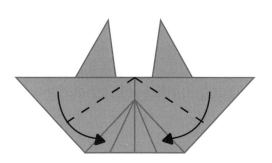

11 Fold along the dotted line.

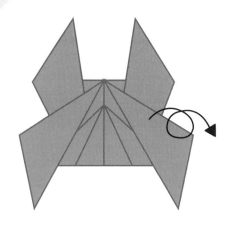

12 Flip over.

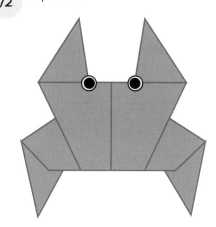

13

Difficulty:

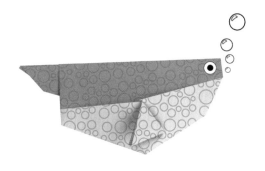

Pufferfish

1 Starting with the darker side up, fold and unfold along the dotted lines.

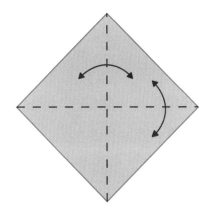

2 Fold inwards along the dotted lines.

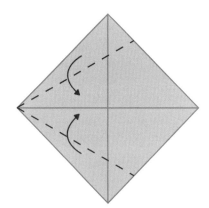

3 Fold inwards along the dotted lines.

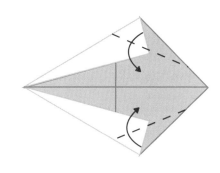

4 Open the top flap to create a pocket and flatten the shape. Repeat on the bottom flap.

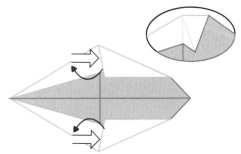

5 Fold inwards along the dotted lines.

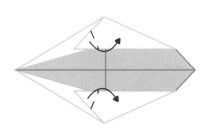

6 Flip over.

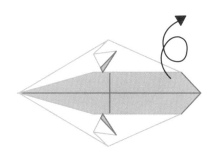

7 Fold inwards along the dotted lines, so the tips meet in the middle.

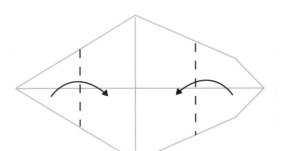

8 Fold back along the dotted line.

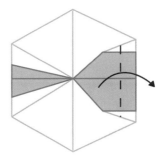

9 Open the inner corners to create pockets and flatten the fold.

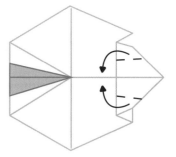

10 Fold in half.

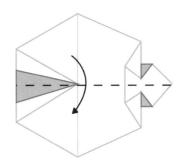

12

11 Fold along dotted line. Repeat the other side.

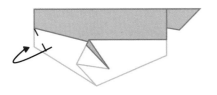

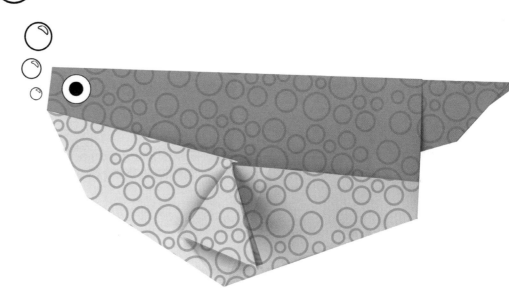

Whale

1. Fold and unfold along the dotted lines.

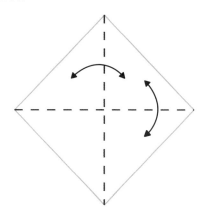

2. Fold top point downwards along the dotted line.

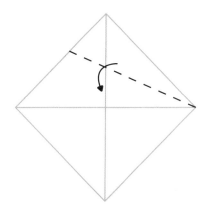

3. Fold and unfold along the dotted line.

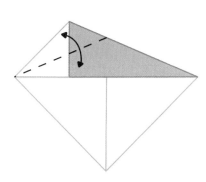

4. Open the flap to create a pocket and flatten the fold.

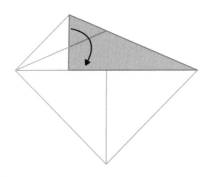

5. Fold the flap you have just created along the dotted line.

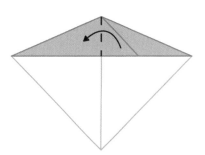

6. Fold inwards along the dotted line.

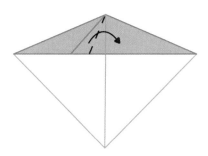

7 Fold backwards along the dotted line.

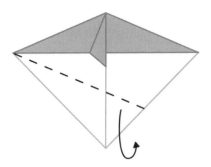

8 Fold backwards along the dotted line.

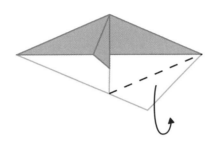

9 Fold backwards along the dotted line.

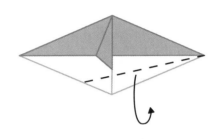

10 Rotate the model to the right a little way.

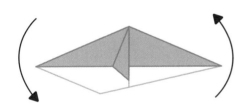

11 Fold the tips backwards, as shown below.

12

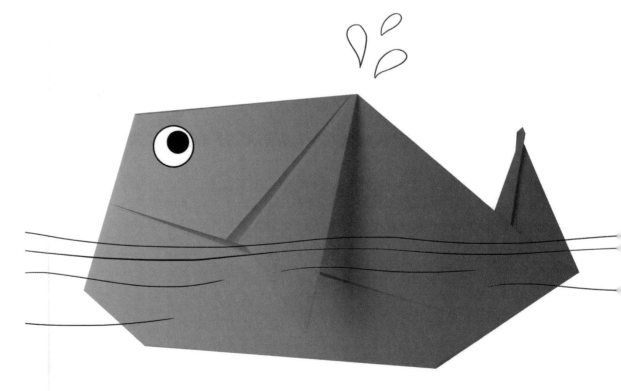

Difficulty: 🦋 🦋 🦋 🦋 🦋

Seahorse

1 Start with light side of paper and fold, then unfold along the two diagonals.

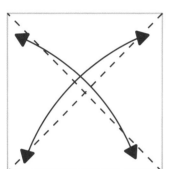

2 Fold inwards along the dotted lines.

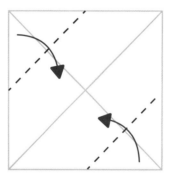

3 Flip over.

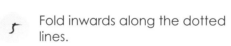

4 Fold inwards along the dotted lines, allowing triangles behind to fold up.

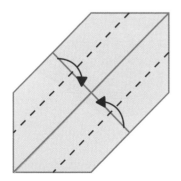

5 Fold inwards along the dotted lines.

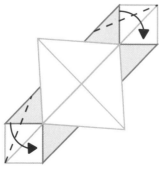

6 Fold inwards along the dotted line.

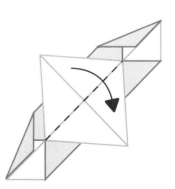

7 Fold and unfold along the dotted line.

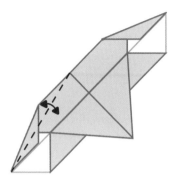

8 Fold upwards along the dotted line.

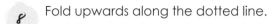

9 Fold and unfold the top tip along the dotted line.

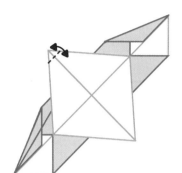

10 Open up the middle corner flaps to create a pocket. Flatten the fold.

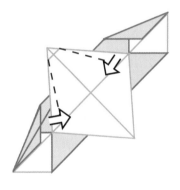

11 Your model should look like this.

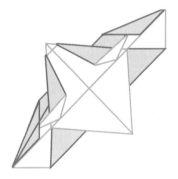

12 Fold along the dotted lines while pushing in the corner to create a fold, as shown below.

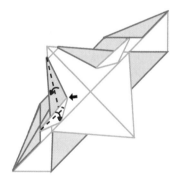

13 Fold inwards along the dotted line.

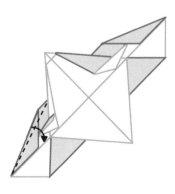

14 Repeat steps 5 to 13 on the other side.

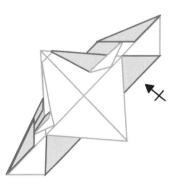

15 Your model should now look like this.

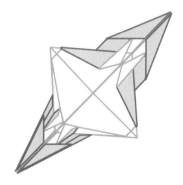

16 Make a crimp fold along the dotted lines.

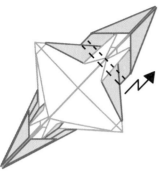

17 Fold the tip behind itself along the dotted line.

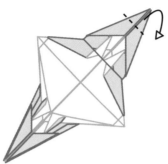

18 Fold behind itself along the dotted line.

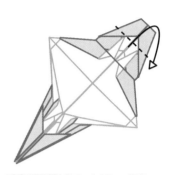

19 Fold the model in half along the dotted line.

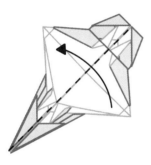

20 Fold tip of the fin behind itself along the dotted line.

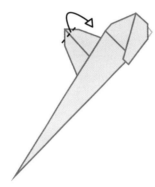

21 Fold tip of the fin behind itself along the dotted line.

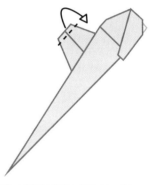

22 Fold the corners of the fin down behind itself.

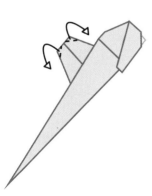

23 Pull the top flap out straight to create the head.

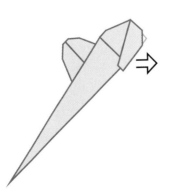

24 Fold along the dotted line. Repeat on the other side.

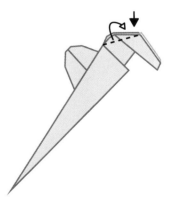

25 Make a squash fold along the dotted lines to define the neck.

26 Make an inside reverse fold along the dotted lines as shown.

27 Curve the tail.

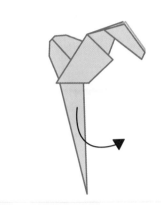

28

Octopus

1 Start with lighter side of the paper. Fold in half along the dotted line.

2 Fold in half again.

3 Open pocket by folding the top triangle to the right.

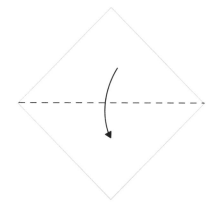

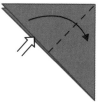

4 Flatten the fold. Flip over.

5 Repeat steps 3 and 4.

6 Lift the top flap and open the pocket. Flatten the fold.

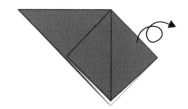

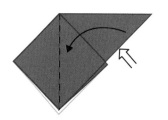

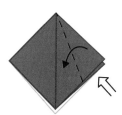

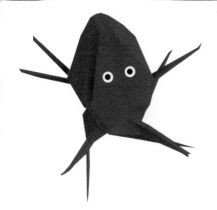

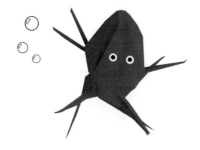

7   Fold pocket up along dotted line. Flatten the fold.

8   Flip over. Repeat steps 6 and 7.

9   Fold flap behind in half. Flip over.

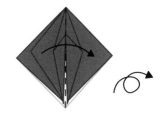

10   Fold flap behind in half and repeat steps 6, 7 and 8.

11   Your model should look like this.

12   Fold along the dotted lines. Flip over.

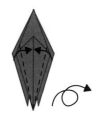

13 Fold along the dotted lines so the corners meet in the middle. Flip over and repeat on the other side.

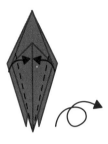

14 Fold flap behind in half.

15 Your model should look like this.

16 Fold along the dotted lines so the corners meet in the middle. Flip over and repeat on the other side.

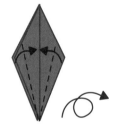

17 Fold upwards along the dotted line. Repeat on the remaining three flaps.

18 Pull the flaps down so they are at 90 degrees to the model. Let the middle unfold to a cube.

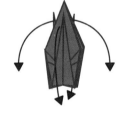

19 Cut each flap along the middle.

20 Valley fold to create eight separate flaps.

21 Blow into the base to inflate the body.

Difficulty:

Turtle

1 Fold and unfold in half horizontally.

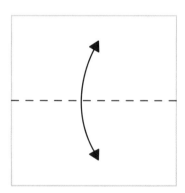

2 Fold and unfold along the dotted lines.

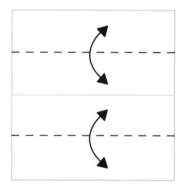

3 Fold and unfold in half vertically.

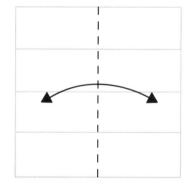

4 Fold and unfold along the dotted lines.

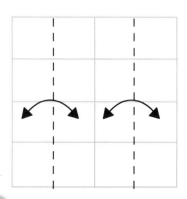

5 Fold and unfold along the dotted lines.

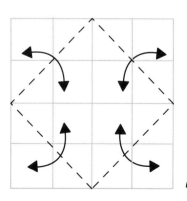

6 Fold and unfold along the dotted lines.

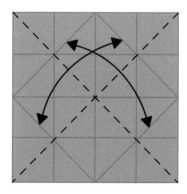

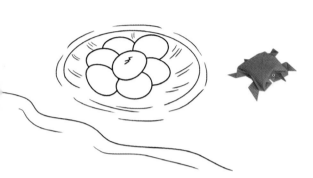

7   Fold the model in half horizontally, while pushing the sides in to create a triangle. Flatten the fold.

8   Lift the bottom flap up while pushing the corners into the middle so the paper folds along the dotted lines.

9   Fold the top point inwards along the dotted line.

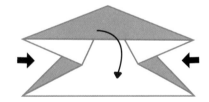

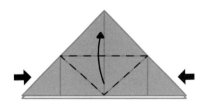

10   Pull the bottom flaps up so they fold along the dotted line as shown below.

11   Flatten the fold.

12   Fold and unfold along the dotted lines.

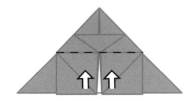

13 Fold inwards along the dotted lines.

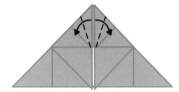

14 Fold inwards along the dotted lines.

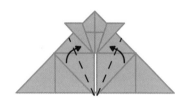

15 Flip over and repeat steps 8 to 14 on the other side.

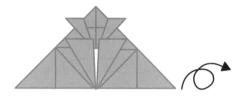

16 Your model should now look like this.

17 Fold in half along the dotted line. Repeat on the other side.

18 Fold upwards along the dotted line. Flip over and repeat on the other side.

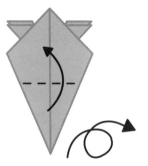

19 Your model should now look like this.

20 Fold in half along the dotted line. Repeat on the other side.

21 Rotate the model so you are looking down on it as shown below.

22 Slowly pull the outer pockets outwards, letting the middle bulge.

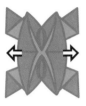

23 Rotate the model 90 degrees.

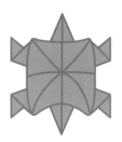

24 Make a reverse fold to create the head.

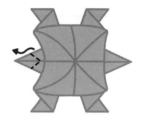

25

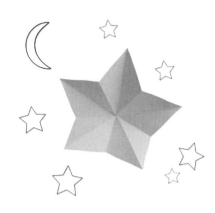

Star

1. Start with the lighter side of the paper. Fold in half.

2. Fold and unfold on the dotted line.

3. Fold and unfold on the dotted line.

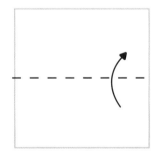

4. Fold to the right on the dotted line.

5. Fold to the left on the dotted line.

6. Fold to the left on the dotted line.

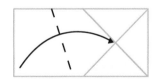

7   Fold backwards along the dotted line.

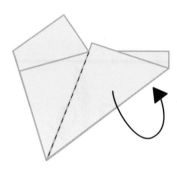

8   Cut with a pair of scissors. Discard the top.

9   Open out the shape.

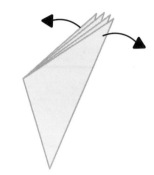

10   Fold to make creases and fold back.

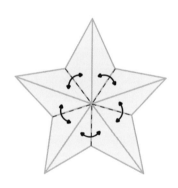

11

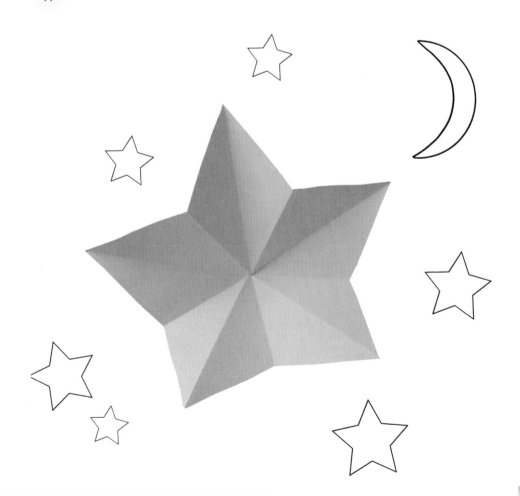

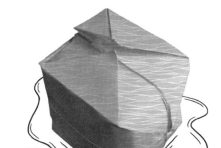

Difficulty:

Water Bomb

1 Fold in half.

2 Fold in half again.

3 Open the bottom left edge and pull towards the right.

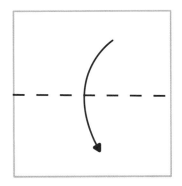

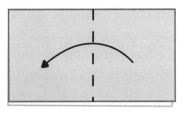

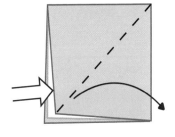

4 Flatten the pocket to create a triangle.

5 Repeat steps 3 and 4 on the other side.

6 Fold upwards along the dotted lines.

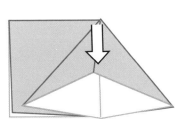

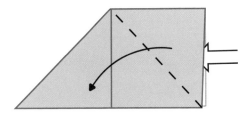

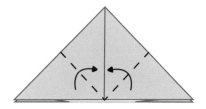

7 Fold backwards along the dotted lines.

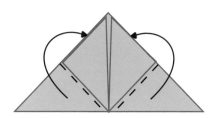

8 Fold inwards along the dotted lines.

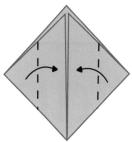

9 Fold backwards along the dotted lines.

10 Pull the top corners downwards.

11 Blow into the model from the bottom point to inflate.

12

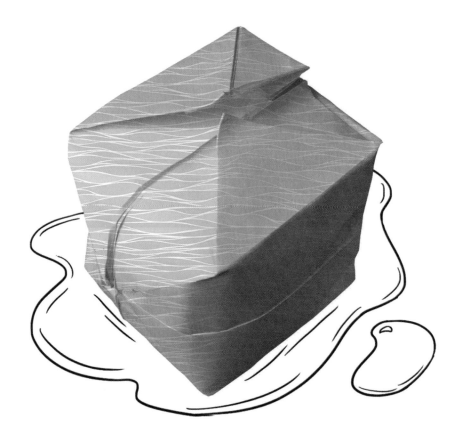

Crane

1 Start with the lighter side of the paper. Fold and unfold along the dotted lines.

2 Fold in half diagonally while pushing the sides inwards.

3 Flatten the fold to create a diamond.

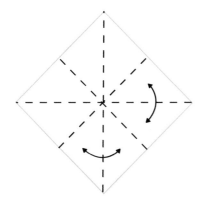

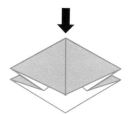

4 Fold and unfold along the dotted lines.

5 Push the flaps inside themselves along the dotted lines and flatten. Flip over and repeat on the other side.

6 Fold along the dotted line. Repeat on the other side.

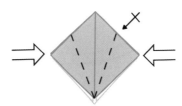

7   Fold along the dotted line. Repeat on the flap behind.

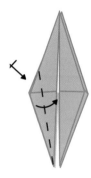

8   Fold top flap along the dotted line.

9   Fold along the dotted line.

10   Fold along the dotted line.

11   Repeat steps 7 to 10 on the other side.

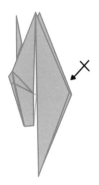

12   Pull tips outwards gently.

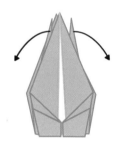

13   Make a reverse fold to create the head.

14   Fold wings down along the dotted line.

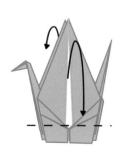

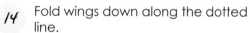

15

Difficulty:

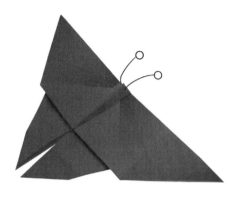

Butterfly

1. Start with the lighter side of the paper. Fold and unfold the paper diagonally.

2. Fold into the center.

3. Turn over.

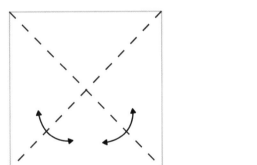

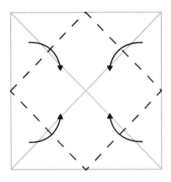

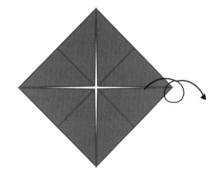

4. Fold and unfold along dotted lines.

5. Turn over.

6. Open out.

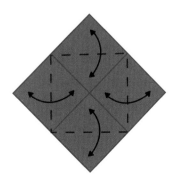

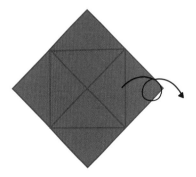

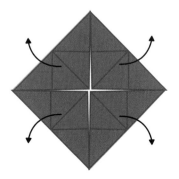

7 Fold along the dotted lines.

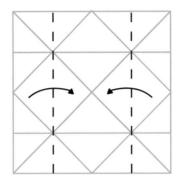

8 Pull out the corners so the paper folds along the dotted lines. Flatten the fold and repeat on the bottom.

9 Fold the model in half behind itself.

10 Fold down along the dotted lines to make butterfly tail.

11 Fold in along the dotted lines.

12 Fold in half along the dotted line.

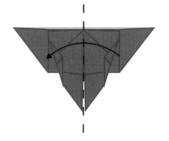

13 Fold along the diagonal dotted line to form the butterfly body.

14 Open out the butterfly's wings.

15

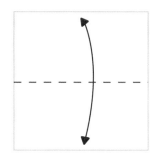
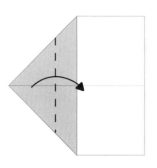

Difficulty:

Jet

1   Start with the lighter side of the paper. Fold and unfold the paper as shown.

2   Fold up the bottom left corner.

3   Fold down the top left corner.

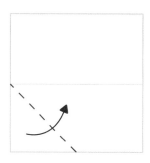
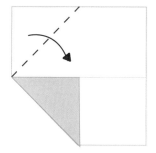

4   Fold back along the dotted line.

5   Fold the nose back on itself.

6   Fold in half along the dotted line to make the wings.

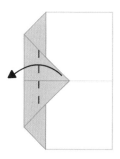
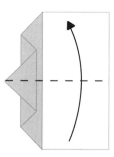

7 Fold down along the dotted line.

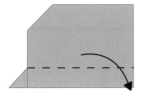

8 Turn over.

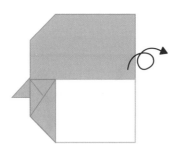

9 Fold down the other wing.

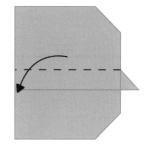

10

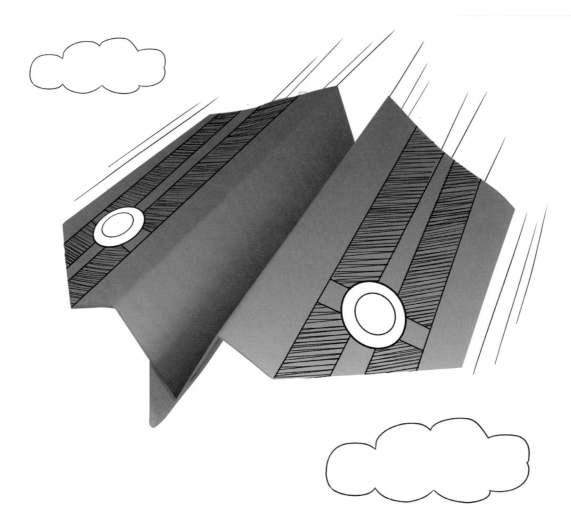

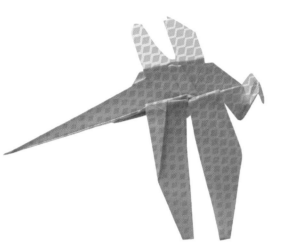

Dragonfly

1 Start with the lighter side of the paper. Fold over along the dotted line.

2 Fold to the left along the dotted line and unfold.

3 Open pocket as shown here and push over to right.

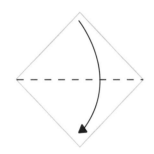

4 Make a pocket and squash flat.

5 Turn over.

6 Make a pocket and squash flat.

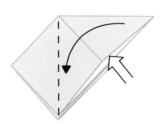

7 Fold and unfold along the dotted lines.

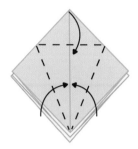

8 Push up along the top fold to create a pocket.

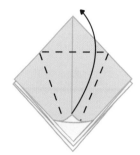

9 Flatten the pocket you have made flat.

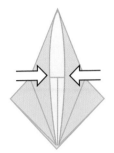

10 Turn over.

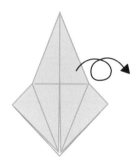

11 Fold down along the dotted line.

12 Turn over.

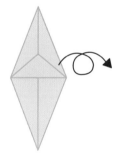

13 Crease along the dotted line.

14 Fold along the dotted line and push up the lower piece from the center.

15 Flatten to look like this. Repeat on the other side.

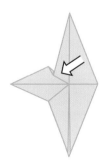

16 Fold in along the dotted line to create a pocket in the corner.

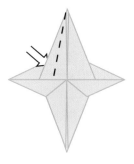

17 Flatten the fold and repeat on the other side.

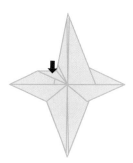

18 Turn over.

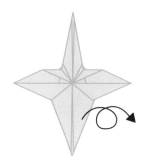

19 Fold in along the dotted line to create a pocket in the corner.

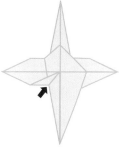

20 Flatten the fold and repeat on the other side.

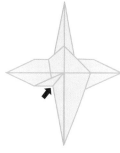

21 Fold the model in half behind itself along the center dotted line.

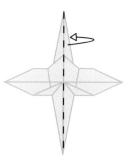

22 Rotate and reverse fold to make the dragonfly's head.

23 Reverse fold along the dotted line.

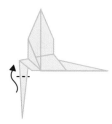

24 Make a reverse fold to finish creating the head.

25 Cut down along dotted line. Repeat on the other side.

26 Make an inside reverse fold on each wing tip.

27 Fold down wings.

28

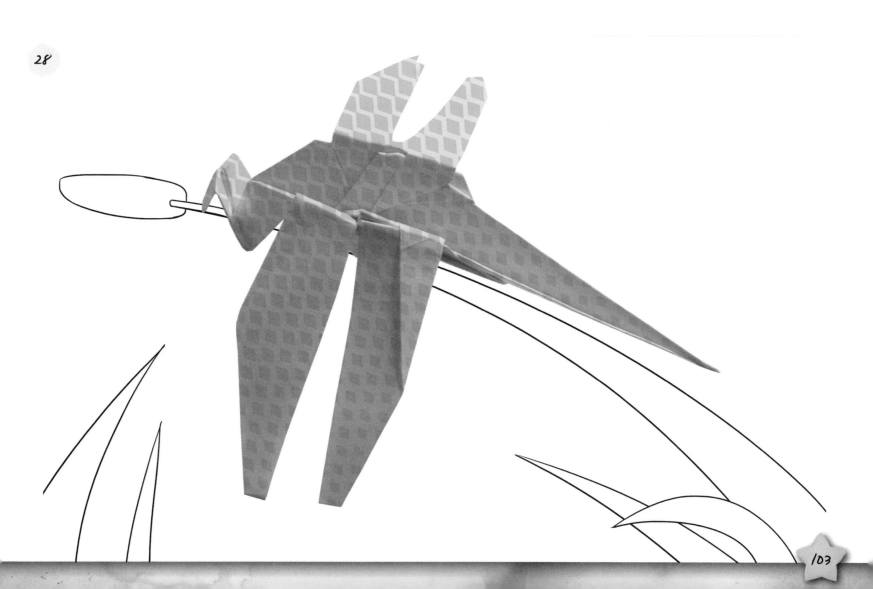

Difficulty:

Hummingbird

1. Start with the lighter side of the paper. Fold and unfold along the dotted lines.

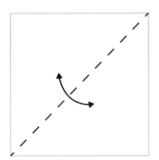

2. Fold and unfold along the dotted lines.

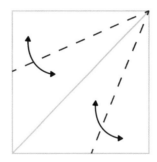

3. Fold over as indicated along the dotted line.

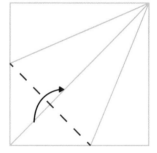

4. Fold in along the dotted lines to form a square.

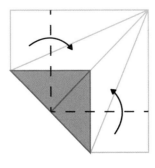

5. Fold along the dotted lines.

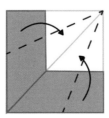

6. Fold down to form a kite shape. Repeat on the other side.

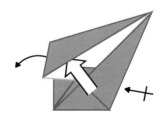

7 Fold up along the dotted lines.

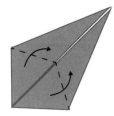

8 Fold over as indicated and repeat for other side.

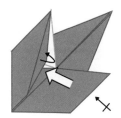

9 Fold over as indicated and repeat for other side.

10 Fold down to form the head.

11 Fold back along dotted line.

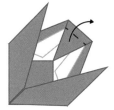

12 Fold up to form beak.

13 Fold in along dotted line.

14 Fold in corners.

15 The head should look like this.

16 Fold down along the dotted line.

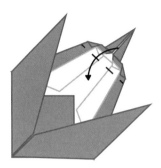

17 Fold along the dotted line to make the body.

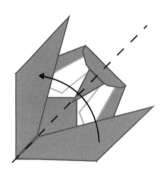

18 Raise the head.

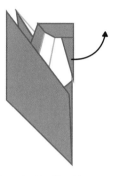

19 Fold down along the dotted line to lower the wings.

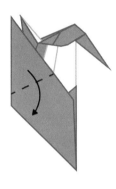

20 Fold at the back of the neck.

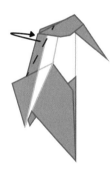

21 Raise up wings.

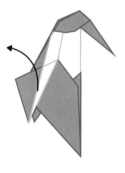

22 Add pleat folds to the wings.

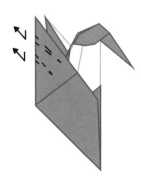

23 Fold back to shape the lower body.

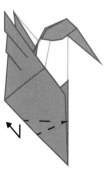

24 Push in to form tail.

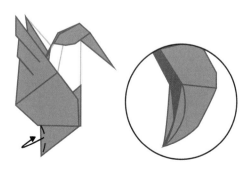

25 Fold in to shape the neck.

26 Give the body a rounded shape.

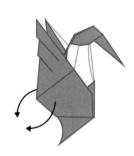

27

Swan

1 Start with the lighter side of the paper. Fold and unfold along the dotted lines.

2 Fold inwards to make a kite shape.

3 Fold behind along the dotted line.

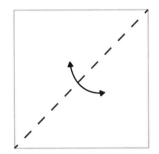

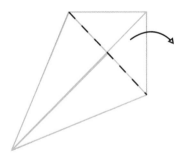

4 Fold and unfold.

5 Fold the left-hand corner inside the flap and flatten to form a diamond shape. Repeat for the right.

6 Your paper should look like this. Turn over.

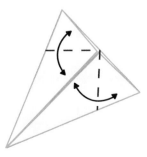

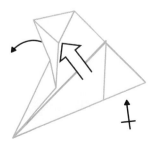

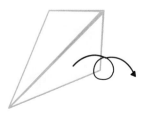

7 Fold up along the dotted line.

8 Fold inwards along the dotted lines.

9 Fold inwards again along the dotted lines.

10 Fold in half along the dotted line.

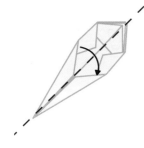

11 Fold down the outer layer.

12 Your model should look like this.

13 Make an inside reverse fold to create a tail.

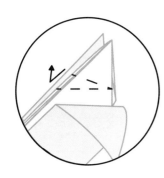

14 Pull the inside point out gently.

15 Fold the outer layer back up.

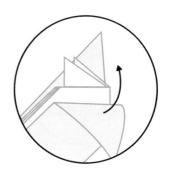

16 Fold back over the body to make the neck.

17 Pleat fold the wing. Repeat on the other side.

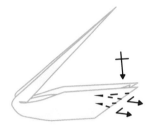

18 Push outwards from the center to give the body volume.

19 Open the bottom layers of the point.

20 Fold down to create the head.

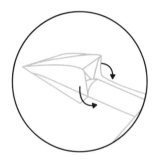

21 Push outwards from the dotted line to create volume.

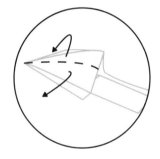

22 Make a crimp fold to create the beak.

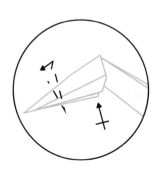

23 Fold the bottom corners under.

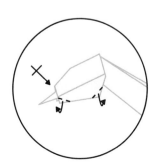

24

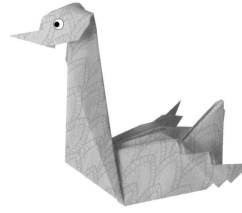

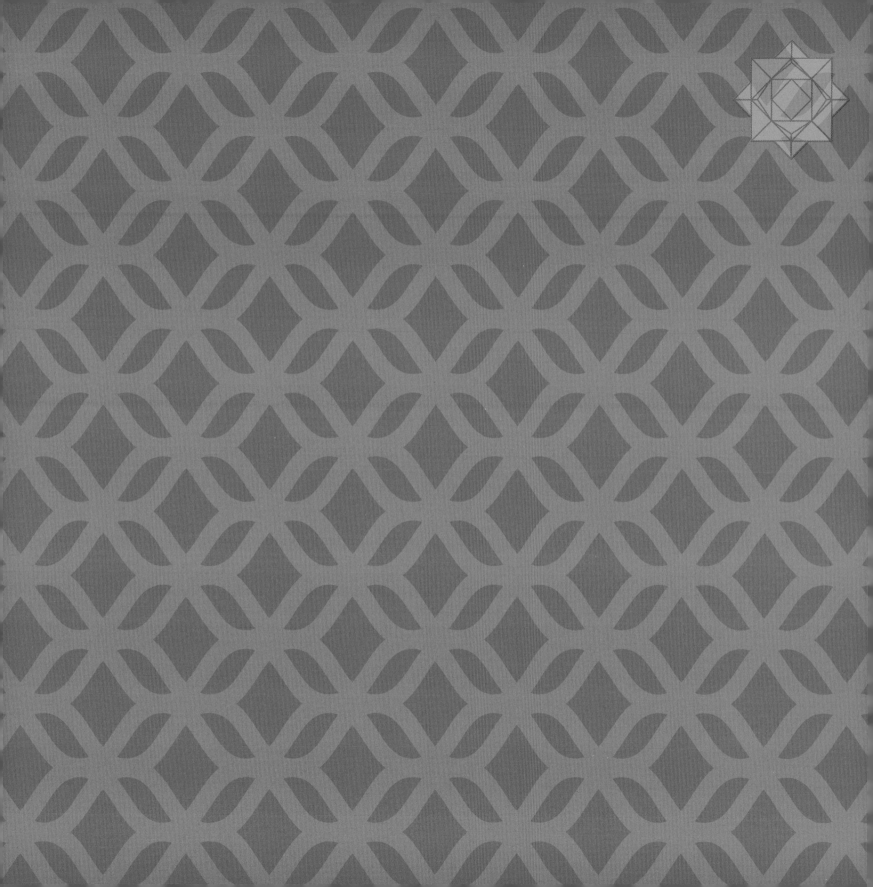

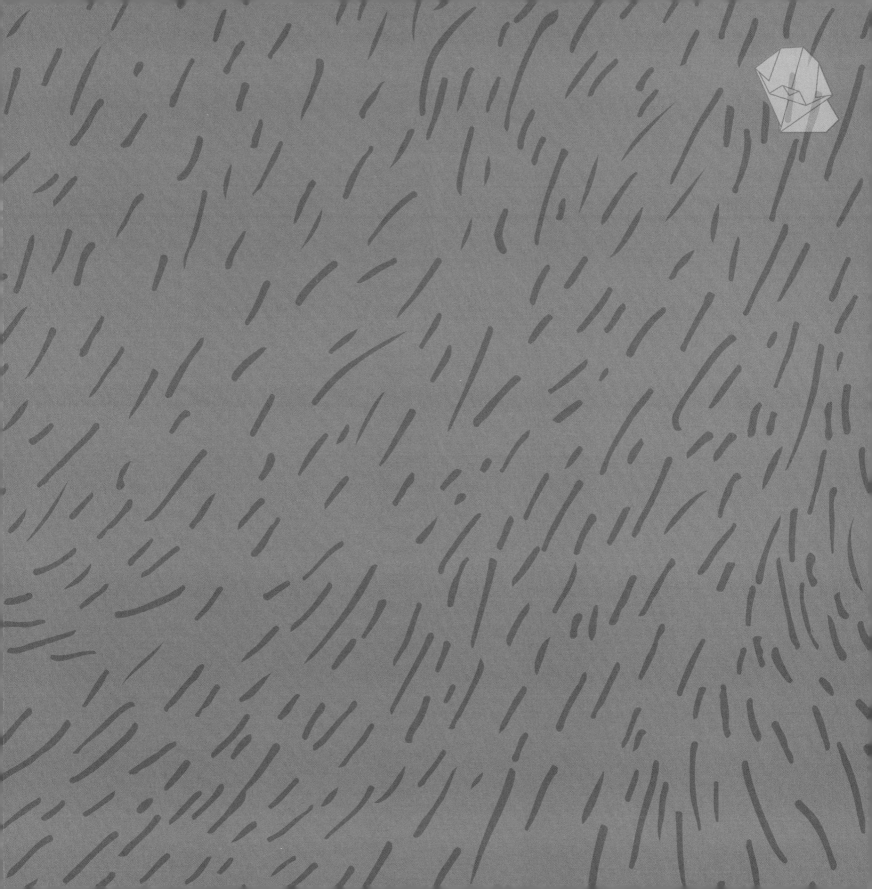

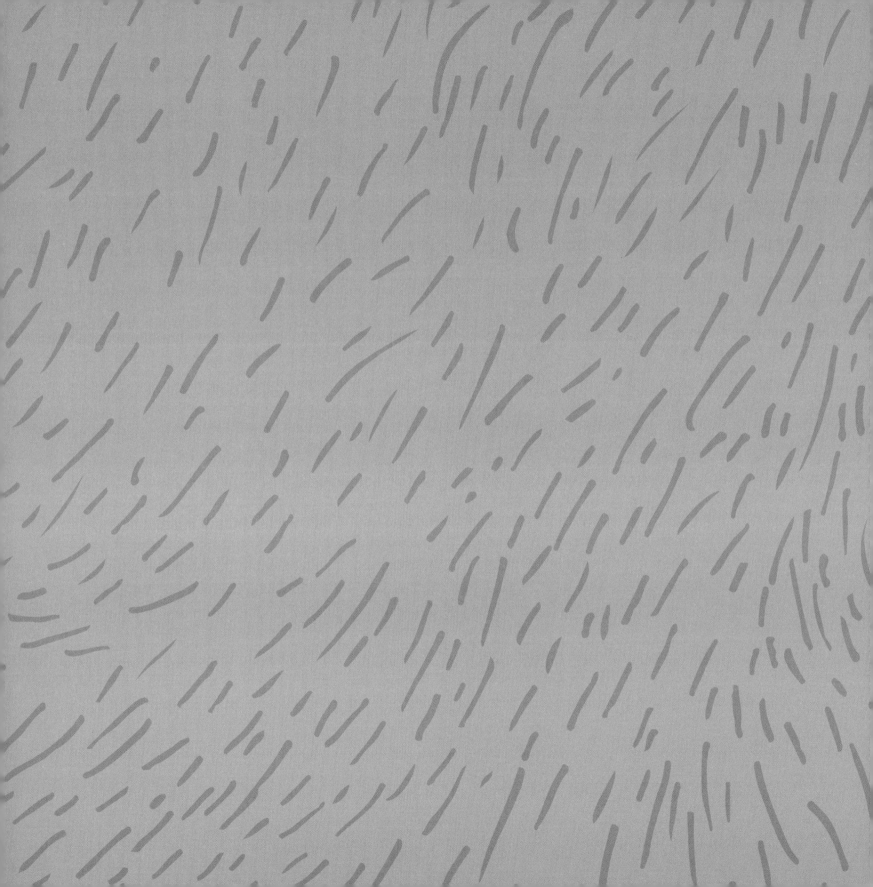

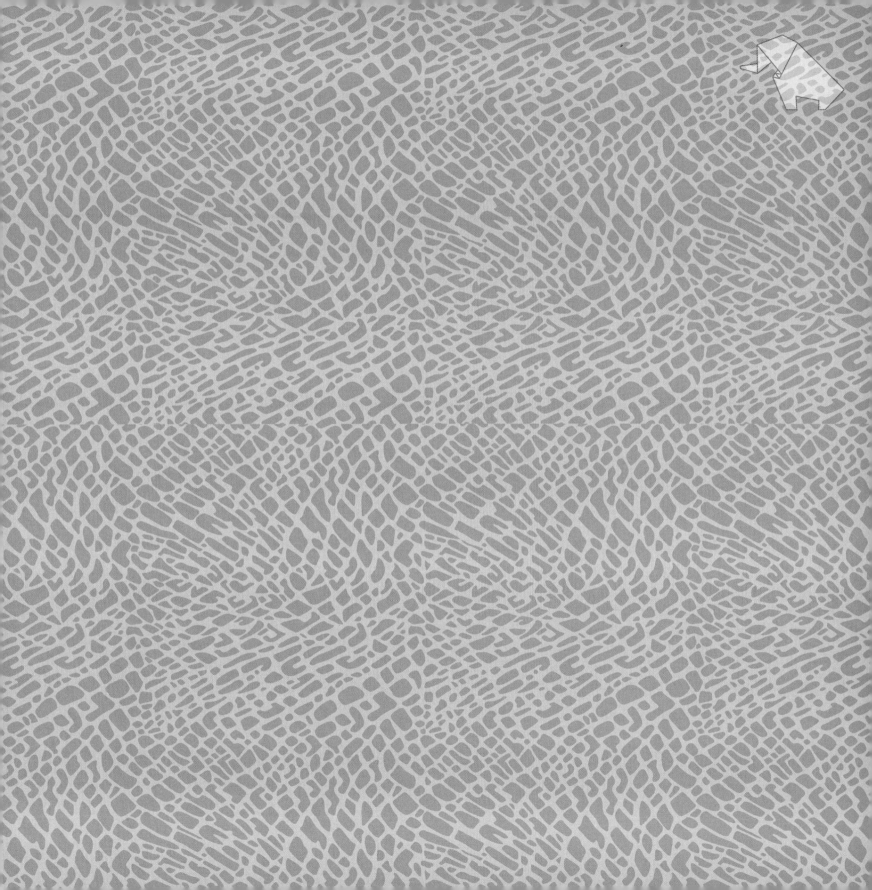

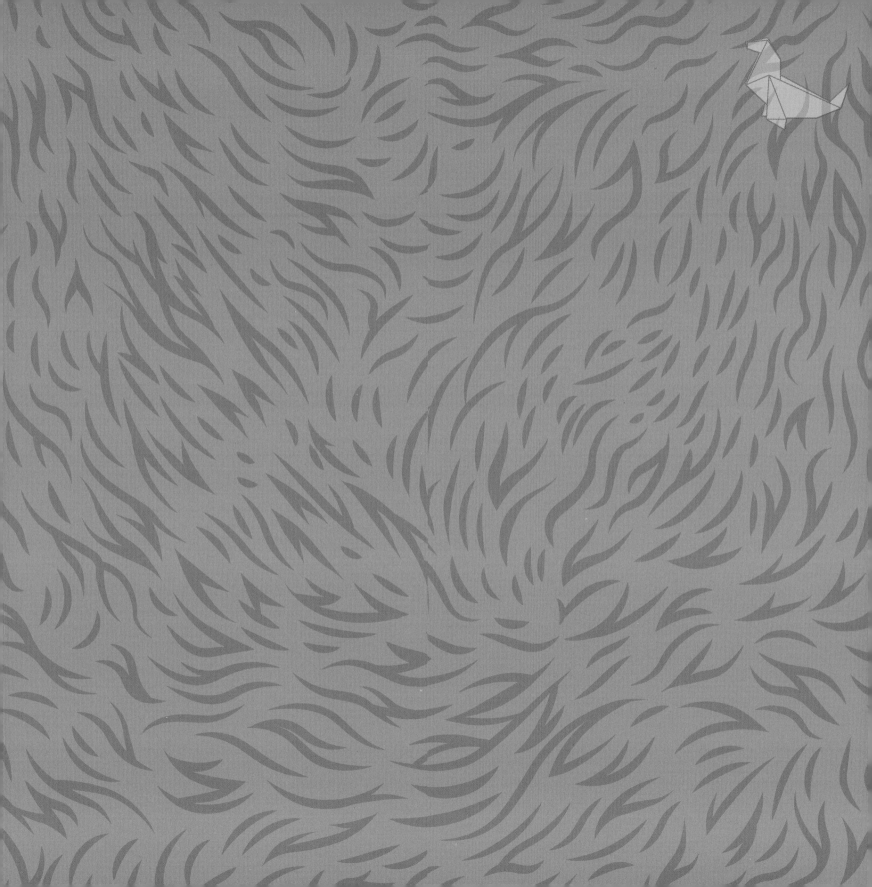

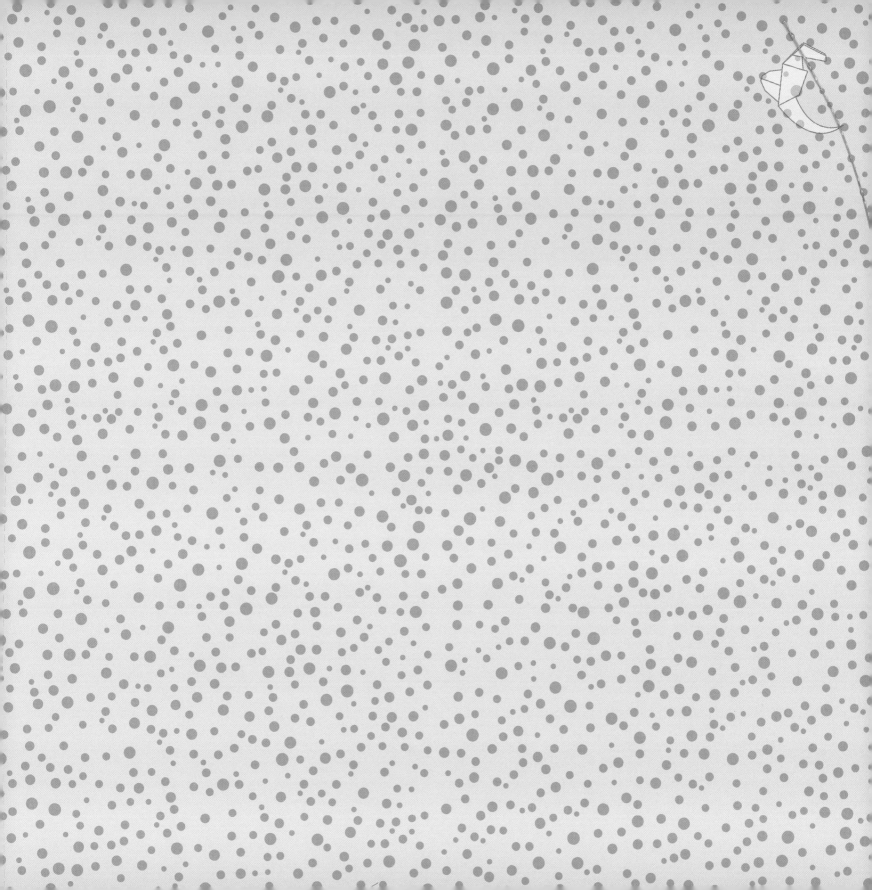

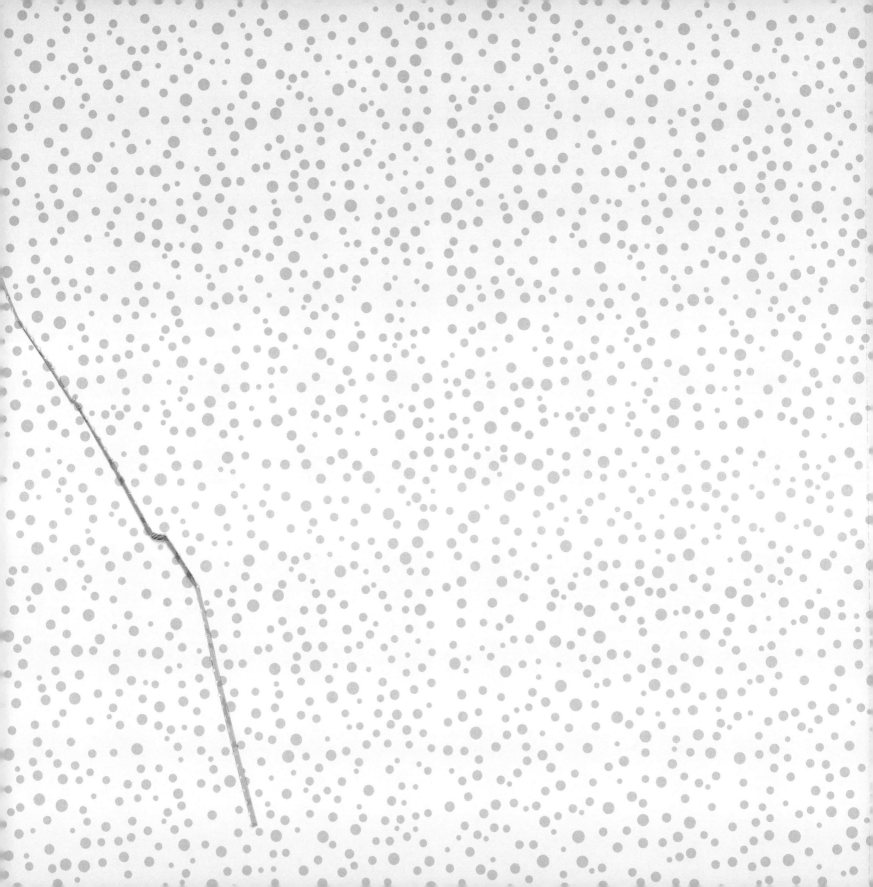

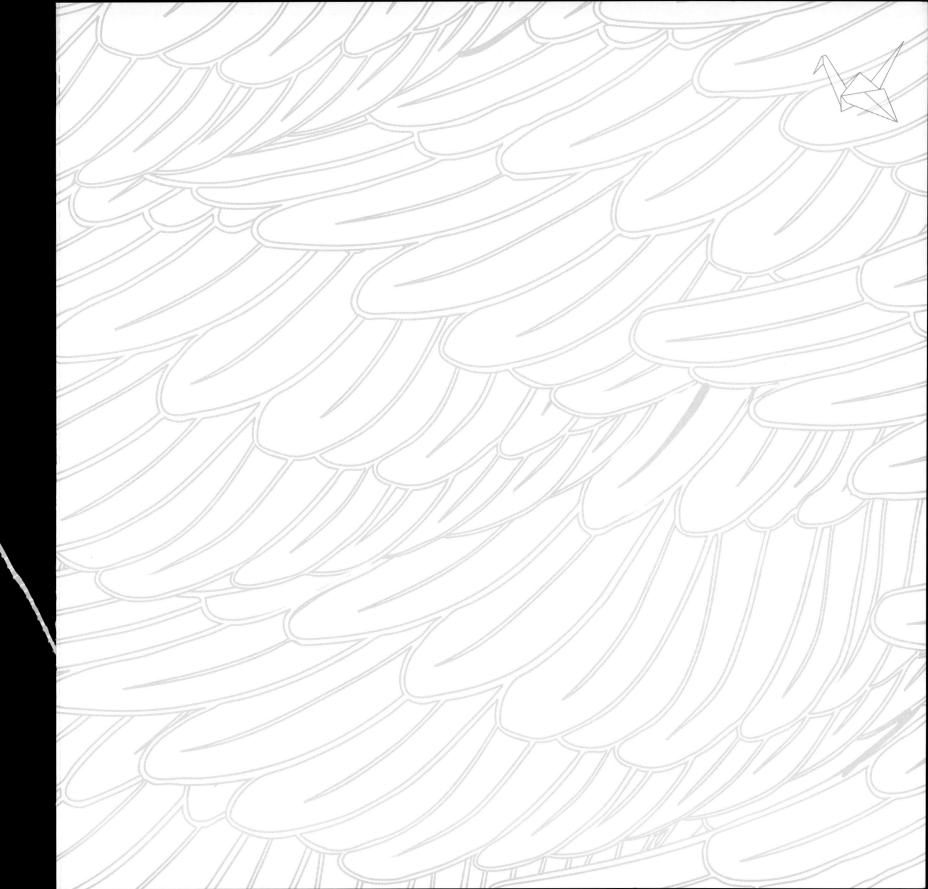

Index